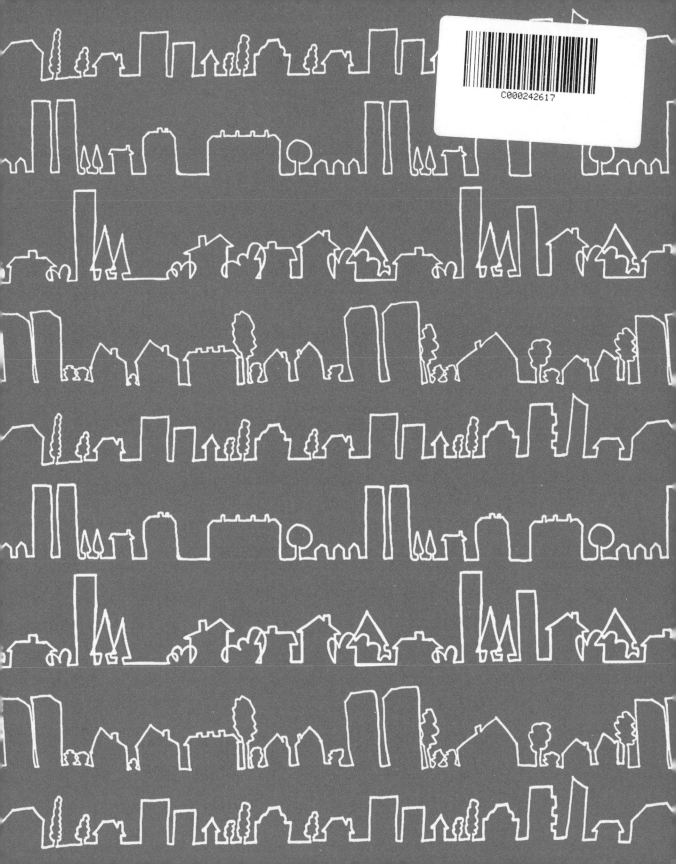

THE ART OF
HOME

A STUDIO PRESS BOOK

First published in the UK in 2021 by Studio Press,
an imprint of Bonnier Books UK,
The Plaza, 535 King's Road, London SW10 0SZ
Owned by Bonnier Books,
Sveavägen 56, Stockholm, Sweden

www.bonnierbooks.co.uk

Text © 2021 Jack March, Joanne Hardcastle, Marie-Claire Jackson and Wendy Simpson
Design © 2021 Studio Press

1 3 5 7 9 10 8 6 4 2

Edited by Stephanie Milton
Designed by Nia Williams
Production by Emma Kidd

A CIP catalogue for this book is available from the British Library
Printed and bound in China

Story Of My Home

THE ART OF
HOME

Interior inspiration for every home

Jack D March, Joanne Hardcastle, Marie-Claire Jackson and Wendy Simpson

STUDIO
PRESS

CONTENTS

1 2 3   1. @tipperleyhill   2. @after_the_fire_2018   3. @carlaelliman
4 5 6   4. @thepajaamahub   5. @alicegraceinteriors   6. @oakappledecor
7 8 9   7. @susiebluesrooms   8. @lara.bezzina   9. @21_holmfield

Welcome to The Art of Home!

First, allow us to introduce ourselves: we are four interior bloggers with a passion for home décor and we found each other online via the Instagram app. You know how we tell children not to talk to strangers on the internet? Well, we did not follow our own advice and boy, are we grateful for that! We're now firm friends and part of an Instagram interiors community called #storyofmyhome.

We created the Story Of My Home account, and this book, to showcase some of the most incredible interiors we've come across (and we've seen a LOT of incredible interiors). We want everyone to feel inspired to make their own home uniquely fabulous, no matter its size and no matter the budget. We know how good it feels to have a little snoop around other people's spaces, so we're going to give you a sneak peek into our own homes, too. In this book we've curated a diverse range of interiors and added our thoughts about each, to get you thinking about ideas for your own space. Next to each photo you'll see the name of the person it belongs to, so you can track them down on Instagram.

When it comes to home interiors, we don't prescribe to a rigid set of rules, or any one style. We don't profess to be interior designers, or experts of any kind, but we each have a distinct style and we know what we like. We believe in picking and choosing elements you love and having fun with your space. If you do this, you'll find that your own unique style will emerge.

So, without further ado, allow us to take you on a tour of the home, starting at the front door…

Joanne, Jack, Wendy and Maz

1 2   1. @hardcastletowers   2. @jackdmarch
3 4   3. @the_yorkshire_homestead 4. @thegingerhareofyorkshire

THE FRONT DOOR

"A front door makes a powerful statement, so we want it to be a positive one. It's a gateway to our home – our sanctuary – and it's what we close when we want to shut the world out."
Maz

"My front door is the equivalent of my face. Irrespective of what's going on inside the house, if you're stood on my front doorstep, all you're going to get is a clean (and usually seasonally styled), warm welcome."
Wendy

"An insight into the people within."

"A smart front door can make your house more saleable. However, this is your home and you'll also want to feel cheerful every time you put your key in the lock, so don't compromise your style."
Joanne

"If you're in an apartment block, shared housing or on a modern housing development with leasehold rules, never fear! I've experienced all of these, and there are still ways to give your door a glow-up."
Jack

FIRST IMPRESSIONS

First impressions count for a lot, and getting your front door aesthetic right is the key to giving the world some insight into the wonderful styling that may lie behind it. It's fairly easy to pull off a good entrance and make your front door stand out from the crowd for all the right reasons.

When choosing colour, consider the style of your property and the materials from which it's built. The door colour should be complementary to the shade of brick. On the colour wheel, complementary colours sit opposite one another and provide a striking contrast. For example, a strong, dark green will look fabulous next to red brick whereas a cyan blue is likely to clash. Pale bricks next to a pastel door could look insipid, so opt for richer, darker colours instead to create a more dynamic aesthetic.

"A lick of paint will take you from tired and drab to absolutely fab in an instant." Wendy

@tipperleyhill   @kelly_prouton

@twyxhouse

Strong, bright colours are not to everyone's taste, however, so if you prefer something a little safer then darker tones are usually a great option. Earthy hues from a neutral palette are classic and timeless.

@homeatthemoat

The aspect of your door will have an effect on the way your chosen colour appears, so get a tester pot before jumping in headfirst. Apply it to a piece of paper and observe how different light levels change its appearance throughout the day. This will give you a good idea of how well your chosen colour will work in practice.

"I'm not an overly superstitious person, but since I bought my last house I've tried to encourage good fortune by painting my front door in a colour that Feng Shui experts suggest is beneficial. My current door faces west, which means I should choose earthy tones. It's currently painted in Farrow & Ball Lichen: a calm, muted green which works well with nature." Maz

If your door is made from a composite material or aluminium, there are many products available that allow you to alter the colour of your door easily. A quick online search or asking at your local DIY store will usually yield some good advice on which products to use.

"Any door worth its salt deserves to be furnished with a beautiful doorknob and knocker, and to be adorned with a bold number, house name or even your own blue plaque!" Joanne

@broomfieldhouserenovation

@making_walford_magical

REPLACING AN OLD DOOR

If you're looking to replace an old door, it's worth considering what era your house was built in, as this will determine the kind of door that will best suit your property. A joiner will be able to advise whether a reclaimed door is suitable if you're looking to pick one up from a salvage yard.

Modern builds tend to have a nod to a certain style, and it's important to consider this when choosing a door. Coloured glass can be a fantastic way to inject some style into the front of your home. Period doors are a wonderful feature and some of the prettiest have elaborate stained glass inserts.

If you aren't a fan of coloured glass, etched glass will also work well. A cost-effective way of achieving a unique look, which will also afford privacy, is to use a patterned film. This is ideal if you like to change things up frequently or are limited by conservation or tenancy restrictions.

@no_9_lake_house

@crack_the_shutters

CURB APPEAL

Curb appeal isn't necessarily about painting your door a bold colour, but rather maintaining a well-kept exterior in general and showcasing your style and personality by creating an eye-catching facade. If you are unable to change your door (for example, if you live in rented accommodation or in a property with strict rules), this is where you get to have a little fun.

There are lots of ways in which you can project your personality onto your home's exterior. A new doormat, potted plants, garden accessories like lanterns and statues or seasonal décor such as hanging baskets and wreaths will all make a huge difference to any property. They will also make you smile every time you arrive home.

A well-placed bench close to the door will offer somewhere to sit as well as creating an area of interest. Place seasonal bedding plants near to it to add cheerful colour throughout the warmer months, as well as depth to your front door aesthetic. This will be easy to maintain all year around if you choose hardy evergreens or topiary bushes.

@feather_and_faff_interiors

@the_yorkshire_homestead

@gillsvictorian

@hearts_at_claremont

Plants can be a great way to draw focus away from the road and onto the property; they're much more fun to look at. If you're planning to landscape the area around your entryway to create a colourful welcome, be sure to leave enough space in the doorway for access so you can comfortably greet visitors. Pretty trees such as olives and bays can look striking in pairs, situated in decorative planters on either side of the door. A pair of olive trees placed outside @hearts_at_claremont's pretty pink door above demonstrates how the addition of some well-chosen plants can elevate the look of your entryway and complement the colour of your front door.

Your front doorstep is the place that links the exterior of your property to the interior, so it makes sense for it to reflect the design of your home and also your interior style. Traditional builds might lend themselves to pretty and relaxed planting designs, while ornamental grasses and structured topiary would sit well outside more contemporary homes. Equally, a pair of pretty topiary bushes will look striking outside an older property.

There are no hard and fast rules, it's all about allowing your imagination to run wild and creating a look that makes your soul sing whenever you turn your key in the lock.

@herhobbithouse

@happeyside

If a less formal aesthetic is your thing, then there are lots of fun door décor ideas you can try. You could go for an eclectic mix of plants and decorative objects, as @herhobbithouse has done above, ensuring that visitors have plenty to look at. Or how about filling wellies with flowers like @happeyside has done? You could also opt for hanging baskets; they are sure to add charm to any doorway. A fun doormat is guaranteed to create a welcoming feel for your guests.

When choosing plants for the front of your property, remember that your front door is a spot where you want to enjoy warm welcomes and happy goodbyes with your friends and family. Any plants with spikes or thorns should be avoided entirely as they're likely to cause issues. Likewise, any plants that are known to attract insects are best avoided, too. It's worth doing your homework here, because no one wants their guests to be scratched, spiked, stung or swarmed when they pay a visit.

Plants need care and attention to keep them healthy, so decking out your entryway with greenery may not appeal to everyone. You can make life easier for yourself by investing in a few key perennials that will flourish for longer periods of time. You can then add further interest throughout the year with a variety of seasonal bulbs which will flower annually.

Climbing plants are another way to enhance the outside of your property and can cleverly disguise mismatched brick where a property has been extended. There are some varieties of climber that can be destructive to the integrity of a building and shoud be avoided, but there are ways to enjoy their immense curb appeal safely. A great way of doing so is to provide a trellis or frame for the plant to cling to. This will allow it to climb without attaching to your wall as it grows. It's important to ensure that climbing plants are never allowed to grow to the height of your eaves or they will start to enter your roof space and dislodge tiles, and could also create a point of access for unwelcome visitors.

SEASONAL STYLING

There's a lot of scope to style up your front door with seasonal accessories. Wreaths are no longer just for Christmas; these days, they are a common sight in every season.

Spring flowers are such a welcome sign of warmer weather to come; a pot of daffodils by the door or a wreath of tulips will brighten even the dreariest spring day. In the UK, Mother's Day occurs in spring in addition to Easter; since both occasions are traditionally celebrated with flowers, this gives you the perfect opportunity to refresh your front door and outside space.

@the_yorkshire_homestead

@no.7_is_home

@the_listed_home

@jpslifeandloves

@thegingerhareofyorkshire

@the_tiny_townhouse

Summer brings with it an abundance of colourful flowers in all shapes and sizes, and it would be a crime not to adorn our doors with them.

The opportunities for summer décor are endless. Why stop at a floral wreath and the obvious planter next to your door when you can pile the blooms up on your steps, or even in your wellies?

@let.there.be.bright

@the_koo_koo_nest_

@jpslifeandloves

@georgianhouseproject

@the.boho.homestead

@hardcastletowers

As soon as the leaves start to fall and you feel that crisp nip in the air, it's pumpkin season. You can arrange them on your doorstep or incorporate smaller pumpkins into a wreath alongside some other autumnal foliage.

Over recent years, it has become a tradition to decorate our doors to celebrate Halloween. This gives you the perfect excuse to have fun with props like skeletons, bats and birds.

@the_koo_koo_nest_

@after_the_fire_2018

@thatssogemma

@gettingstuffdoneinheels

@house_of_glebe

@jackdmarch

Next comes Diwali with bright, colourful rangoli designs, closely followed by Chanukah with its candles, and the midwinter tradition of evergreen wreaths.

The festive season shouts out for devastatingly beautiful door décor, and it's the perfect time to push the boat out. Baubles and sparkles are the perfect addition to your front door décor.

@georgianhouseproject

@ahometomakeyousmile

@wiltshirewonderland

@niathebookdesigner

@thatssogemma

@the_yorkshire_homestead

TEN FRONT DOOR COMMANDMENTS

1. Maintaining a well-kept exterior makes your home look fresh and inviting.

2. The colour of your brick or exterior will help to determine what colour door will best suit your house.

3. Applying paint from a tester to a small piece of paper or wood and temporarily fixing it in place will give you a good idea of how your choice of colour will work.

4. Aluminium and composite doors can be painted with the right preparation and products.

5. There are lots of bold options for door furniture. Add interest with a beautiful door knocker, numbers or lettering.

6. Consider the period of your property when choosing a replacement front door.

7. Consult with your joiner or builder to see if it's possible to install a reclaimed door.

8. Doors with glazed panels allow light to shine through into the hall or entrance.

9. Etched glass will offer privacy in glazed panels.

10. If you are restricted by contract or conservation regulations, use moveable embellishments like a decorative doormat and potted plants or topiary.

@catwalktocowpat

@after_the_fire_2018

THE HALLWAY

"This is the area that connects the whole house, so it's important to have cohesion here: carefully chosen elements that tie everything together in the space to make it a room in its own right."
Joanne

"While I'm of the opinion that a hallway should always be visitor-ready, that should not stop it being a functional space. You just have to be clever with your storage solutions."
Jack

"Often small, but always a hardworking space."

"In my home, the hallway is a high-traffic area and experience has taught me to choose the décor very carefully! I recently painted my staircase and now it's a lot easier to keep clean than my old cream carpet."
Maz

"There isn't a hallway on earth that doesn't struggle to contain shoe and coat overspill effectively. Not to be overlooked as a corridor, the hallway is a vital room that sets the tone for the rest of your home."
Wendy

MAKING THE MOST OF YOUR SPACE

For most people, the hallway isn't a grand, open space, and for those in apartments or bungalows it's unlikely to have a staircase. However, that doesn't make it any less important. The hallway is the anchor for the home, with the majority of the rooms leading off it.

@cynthiamargaretathome

@banish_the_beige_

@cloud_nine_interiors

Small hallways can still be styled and decorated to create a little slice of grandeur; they just need to work a little harder than bigger hallways. A large mirror can work wonders in a small hall: not only does it give the space a sense of importance, it also serves a practical function as it allows you to check your appearance on the way out of the front door! Most importantly, it helps to bounce the light around the space, creating the illusion of a bigger room.

The choice of furniture in small hallways is an important consideration. When considering a piece, ask yourself: is it practical, and does it bring anything to the space? It's about getting creative and clever with your choices.

While large, open hallways may comfortably house a mirror with a nice console table underneath, complete with special drawer for keys, in a smaller hall a narrow cabinet may be a better choice as it provides more storage space for things like umbrellas and shoes. In a narrow hall, a simple shelf above a radiator provides a space to indulge in a bit of styling.

STORAGE

No matter the shape and size of your hallway, one thing will always be true: without an adequate storage solution for shoes, coats and bags, this room can quickly become an untidy dumping ground.

You might think boot rooms are only for the largest of dwellings, but you can introduce a boot room aesthetic to a smaller hallway or porch, and incorporate practical yet stylish storage solutions.

If you are lucky enough to have high ceilings, you can maximise your storage potential by taking a vertical approach to cabinets and shelving. If you have lower ceilings you can still achieve a boot room feel by placing a small shelf for pretty storage baskets above coat hooks. Wicker baskets will add texture and interest to the area, and are an ideal way to store smaller accessories, keeping the space clear and clutter free. A second row of coat hooks placed lower down the wall is ideal for children and will ensure they can access their own coats and bags.

@mrs_k_at_the_bridge

@wiltshirewonderland

Come As You Are

Winter

A bench will provide somewhere comfortable for you to sit while you remove footwear. If you're looking to maximise storage, consider an ottoman-style bench with a lift-up lid, or add shelving below your bench.

The area under the stairs can provide a useful storage space, but it's an awkward shape and all too often it becomes a messy area, making its contents difficult to access. That's where under stair drawers come in: they're functional, user-friendly and easy to keep tidy. Never again will you experience the back-breaking struggle of hunting for a lost shoe in the cupboard under the stairs.

@sissinghurstlocationhouse

@buildingthemushroom

@tiffyandflow

DRAMATIC DÉCOR

Many hallways have a large expanse of wall, providing you with the perfect spot to create that gallery wall you've always dreamed of. An eclectic collection of artwork lends itself perfectly to awkward, narrow spaces, and is a sure-fire way to inject some of your personality into the hallway. Don't be afraid of grouping a wide array of artwork together, mixing vintage charity shop finds with modern typography to create a gallery that's personal to you. Add other items in to create interest such as plates, vintage letters or signs. Another way to inject drama would be to adorn the wall with a mural created using durable paints.

It wouldn't be wise to use delicate finishes with a high price tag to enhance your hallway, as it sees so much traffic. But that doesn't mean you can't inject interest: simply incorporate well-designed, functional pieces of hardware such as coat hooks, handles and elaborate light fittings to bring more personality to the space in a practical way.

@sallydoessassy

@jessjones.the_art_room

@broomfieldhouserenovation

FLOORS AND WALLS

When it comes to hallway flooring, it makes sense to opt for something that scrubs up nicely as it's going to see a lot of traffic. That's not to say you can't have a lovely stair carpet: just make sure you avoid a colour that will show the tell-tale sign of a busy thoroughfare. Hard flooring such as tiles and natural woods are easy to keep clean, and vinyls and laminates have come a long way and are perfect for this hard-working room.

It would be a risky business to showcase eye-wateringly expensive wallpaper in this high-traffic area, because the walls will inevitably fall victim to scuffs and dirt splashes. Panelling and lincrusta are enjoying a revival, no doubt thanks to their robust yet decorative qualities.

The hallway is also a great room in which to splash out on some wipeable paint. There are a number of brands that offer either 'diamond hard' or scrubbable options which will cost slightly more than standard emulsions but will pay dividends in the long run.

1 2
3
4

1. @prettyprospectcottage   3. @flamingostyling
2. @homeatthemoat   4. @hardcastletowers

STOP AND STAIR

The staircase provides you with the perfect opportunity to make a statement and create drama. An eye-catching stair runner or carpet may be just the thing: sisal is hardwearing, stripes are classic and animal print is striking.

Painted stairs are cheaper, provide an equally hardwearing finish and are easier to clean. There's so much scope to add interest with pattern, stencils or even gold leaf. Prepare the surface well and be sure to prime and undercoat first, then seal with a few coats of varnish to ensure a hardwearing finish. Remember to paint every other step so you can use them while waiting for the paint to dry.

You can also make a statement with your bannister. Consider embracing the natural timber, or be daring and go for a bright, bold pop of colour.

1
2 3 4

1. @somethingbluehome   2. @chiclecticblog
3. @pebbles_and_peanuts   4. @indigoleopardhome

1 2 3
4 5 6

1. @kate_rose_morgan   2. @paintthetownpastel   3. @mysecondhandhouse
4. @ahometomakeyousmile   5. @violetmay38   6. @carlaelliman

@annalysejacobs

TEN HALLWAY COMMANDMENTS

1. Mirrors can add light and drama to a small space.

2. Radiator shelves provide a perfect ledge to style in narrow hallways.

3. If you have a high ceiling, take a vertical approach to shelving to make the most of the wall space.

4. Consider using the space under the stairs to maximise storage potential.

5. The hallway is the perfect place to showcase your art collection as a gallery wall.

6. A mural is a fun way to inject personality.

7. Incorporate well-designed, functional hardware to add style and functionality.

8. Opt for a hardwearing floor that's easy to maintain.

9. Scrubbable paint costs slightly more than standard emulsions but will pay dividends in the long run.

10. A budget-friendly way to add impact on the staircase is to use paint.

@justices_nest

THE LIVING ROOM

"I think it's probably my favourite room because it's where I relax at the end of the day. I've filled it with pieces of furniture in sumptuous velvets. In an ideal world I'd ban teenagers because they can be clumsy with food and drink..."
Maz

"The living room is the place where I showcase my statement and favourite pieces. From whimsical teapots to treasured antiques, each tells a story while reflecting my personality."
Jack

"A cosy retreat in which to unwind."

"I love the idea of a room to retreat to and snuggle down in. The living room is my sanctuary from the hurly-burly of everyday life and a place to relax and unwind."
Joanne

"Ours is reserved purely for special occasions or surprise visits! It remains a perpetually tidy and well-preserved space to cash in on, as and when we need it."
Wendy

THE SOFA

A sofa, settee or couch (whichever you prefer) is often considered the linchpin of the living room. It's where you snuggle down with friends and family to watch a movie, or where you sit in solitude in your pyjamas as you work your way through the latest box set. Naturally, comfort and durability are the key things to consider when selecting your sofa, and many people opt to stay clear of cream if they have pets and/or a growing family.

"I saved for ages to buy it: a big, cream, linen sofa that you could sink into with a good book and a piping hot mug of tea, providing you're not clumsy. Oh, and you couldn't even think about going near it with fake tan, red wine or chocolate; you'd have to sit on the floor instead." Jack

A great way to get some insight into the durability of a sofa before you purchase it is to search for your desired brand on selling sites. Looking at second-hand pieces will show you how the fabrics and cushion inners are likely to wear over time.

Talking of fabric, sofas have come a long way since the days when your only options were embossed velour, leather or linen. Now there's a long list of materials, including technologically-advanced easy-clean velvet and linen, giving you plenty of options as well as peace of mind. And the colour spectrum has also evolved; many brands now boast an entire rainbow colour palette.

1. @thiscolourfulnest   2. @after_the_fire_2018
3. @hornsby_style   4. @a_story_of_home
1 2 3   5. @my.interior.tales   6. @fallingforfilberts
4 5 6   7. @thepajaamahub   8. @houseofharnasz
7 8 9   9. @thiscolourfulnest

PRACTICAL VERSUS PRETTY

If you have the luxury of a more formal living room that isn't used every day, your curtains can be puddled and you can order your snuggle chair in a totally impractical velvet fabric. Sadly, these wonderfully sumptuous finishes would most likely fall victim to everyday life in a family room, so they aren't for everyone.

"When I think of a living room, I think of the place I want to relax. When my children were younger, we were lucky enough to have space for them to play in another room. Our living room was not the room where we threw the cushions on the floor to make dens (well, not too often, anyway). It was not the place for food or drinks, except maybe a weekend treat of popcorn and hot chocolate. Obviously this rule was relaxed after the children had gone to bed so we could enjoy a G&T or a glass of red."
Joanne

Fortunately, there are ways to merge practical and pretty. If you're raising a family or you're a lover of animals, go for key pieces that will age well but still reflect your style. Invest in fabric protection so that the inevitable spills can be easily remedied. As our families grow up, our living space evolves, and making clever choices will ensure that investment pieces will withstand the test of time. Think about hardwearing fabrics and surfaces that are scratch and stain resistant.

For family-friendly style smarts, opt for wall lighting like @designermumetc has done in her living room. This will free up surface space and protect your lights from sticky fingers and dirty paws.

@designermumetc

@houseofharnasz

@tale_of_a_terrace

STORAGE

Build shelves and cupboards into alcoves to maximise storage space and ensure toys and other clutter can easily be put away when guests arrive or you're ready for some downtime. Be sure to utilise the whole wall right up to the ceiling; even in a room with a low ceiling, you'll give the illusion of height while also creating a safe space up high where you can display your most precious or sentimental objects.

If you don't have alcoves to build into, look for tall, slim pieces of furniture that can work extra hard as storage while also providing a surface for plants or anything else that deserves to be showcased out of harm's way. It's important to stabilise items of furniture that could be prone to tipping – this should be done by firmly securing them to a wall.

If your living room is a place where young children play, floor space will be key. Go for a nest of tables that can be tucked up together and then opened out when you need them as opposed to one large coffee table that will fill the space.

@story_behind_the_stone

@oldrectonewoldrec

GETTING COSY

Think of the living room as a place to retreat to and snuggle down in: a sanctuary away from the chaos of everyday life. Colour, pattern and texture are crucial elements of any room design but are particularly important when you're trying to create a cosy spot.

Texture is how something feels, and will dictate how a room is perceived, as well as giving a room more depth. Pattern is about the visual surface design. When trying to create a relaxing space, consider soft, luxurious finishes such as deep carpets, plump velvet cushions and cosy woollen throws. Layering these up will create contrast, which is a trick used to balance the design; it provides a visual interest and is achieved by mixing hard and soft textures, as well as a variety of colours and patterns.

@thepajaamahub

@victoriaaldersonart

The lighting must be versatile; sometimes it'll need to be functional, at other times relaxing. Make sure all aspects are covered: you'll want an overhead light, table lamps and candlelight, so you have an option for every occasion. In order to turn your living room into a real retreat, all senses must be catered for, so it's got to smell delicious, too. This is the room where you should burn your best candles; choose relaxing, soothing smells that reflect the season and time of year.

@ourvictoriandetached

@pink_rucksack

BIG FURNITURE DRAMA

"I lived in apartments for many years, and my living space didn't have a traditional focal point like a fireplace or a lovely bay window. With this in mind, I was conscious that I did not want the television to be the focal point. I solved this by making the sofa the principal piece that drew the eye." Jack

A common misconception is that large, statement pieces of furniture have no place in small rooms, but that simply isn't true. In reality, a beautiful sideboard can create useful storage and a focal point in a small space, as well as in a new build that lacks a fireplace.

A large, ornamental, statement mirror like the one we see here in @charlmidwife's living room will add drama to any space. It will also help to bounce light around the room, giving the illusion of space where it's needed most.

Let's talk about the elephant in the room: the television. It's certainly not the most attractive feature in any living space, but most of us like to own at least one television, and many of us appreciate the guilty pleasure of a box set binge from time to time. It's part of everyday life and it's here to stay, so we need to find some clever ways to minimise its impact on your interior design.

@charlmidwife

@sarahstricky

"There was a MASSIVE debate when we moved into our current house. We have a sitting room off the kitchen that boasts a huge TV, where every man and his (many) dogs sit. I wanted our living room to be a grown-up space, full of precious things and sumptuous furnishings that weren't blighted by the presence of a 40-inch flatscreen." Wendy

A large TV will often overpower and dominate a space, so a good solution is to create designated TV storage, thereby turning this unattractive item into more of a feature. You can achieve this through the clever use of shelving, with one space dedicated to the TV. Items placed on the other shelves around the TV create interest, drawing the eye away from the screen.

@jackdmarch

If you paint the wall around the TV in a dark shade, it will help camouflage the screen. When the TV is turned off, it disappears into the background. You could also conceal your TV as @theresa_gromski has done, by hanging a light canvas over it when it isn't in use – you'd never know it was there!

Another clever solution is to sink the TV into a wall so that it's flush with the surroundings and all those unsightly wires are hidden from view. Bear in mind that a wall doesn't have be built out of plasterboard; you can use cheaper materials like MDF. Integral shelving added below the TV can house any additional electrical equipment such as games consoles and TV boxes.

@theresa_gromski

@thegingerhareofyorkshire

A brief word on TV location in relation to your health: position is key and a well-placed TV will enhance your viewing experience and help you to avoid straining your neck.

"Many years ago, I was told by a chiropractor that people often unknowingly develop or exacerbate neck injuries by watching television at the wrong angle. Since this revelation I try to ensure our TV is placed in a direct line with a chair or sofa so that no one develops a cricked neck on my watch." Maz

TEN LIVING ROOM COMMANDMENTS

1. Hunt for sofa brands you like on selling sites to see how they wear with age.

2. Look for advanced, easy-clean fabric options for sofas and soft furnishings, or consider treating them with fabric protector to safeguard against accidental spillages.

3. Utilise the wall right up to the ceiling to maximise storage space and give the illusion of height.

4. Precious treasures should not be hidden away. Display them in safe spots for all to see; they usually look best in odd numbers.

5. Remember that you must always secure large, tall furniture to the wall.

6. Layer different luxurious textures, such as velvet and faux fur, to give a sumptuous, relaxing vibe.

7. To help you create the ultimate cosy retreat, think about all your senses when planning your living room.

8. If you don't have a fireplace, use a large piece of furniture as a focal point, or install a mantle shelf.

9. Create built-in storage to make your TV less prominent.

10. Paint the space behind your TV in a darker shade to help it blend into the space when not in use.

@onealchemyhouse

@alicegraceinteriors

THE DINING ROOM

"The dining room is a fabulous but largely dormant room in our house. It's a lovely thing to have and really comes into its own at Christmas and Easter: our family's two main feasting celebrations."
Wendy

"I need to feel able to eat a solitary plate of baked beans in my dining room, with the newspaper, as well as squashing the whole family around the table for a celebratory feast full of laughter and candlelight."
Joanne

"A space to gather together."

"For years my dining room was the small breakfast bar in my open-plan apartment, and while it may have been a tight squeeze, it holds many wonderful memories."
Jack

"It's rare these days to have the luxury of a room designed for the sole purpose of eating, so I think dining rooms in the strictest sense have given way to more multi-functional spaces. That's certainly true in my house."
Maz

THE HEART OF THE HOME

The dining room is often the heart of the home. Not everybody has an actual room, but most people will have a table, or a spot where the family gathers to eat. As well as being a place where we enjoy a meal with friends and family, the dining area is central to the ebb and flow of family life. Over the years, it might see children sitting around it scribbling with crayons, doing jigsaws, learning to write, studying for SATS, GCSEs, A-levels and degrees. For many people, it also has to double as a home office.

@brush_up_dress_down

@kylamagrathinteriors

A lived-in, everyday family dining space can easily be given a glow-up for a special occasion with the addition of a few choice props. Candlelight and lamps will soften the lighting and help to create an ambient mood. The right linen will elevate a scrubbed table into something far grander. Tablecloths and runners are easy to find, but crushed velvet and other fabrics can be bought by the metre relatively inexpensively, and will add a wow factor for a special occasion. Collect crockery in matching or contrasting tones to build up a perfect dining service; make sure you keep your eyes peeled in charity shops. Think of a theme or colour that you enjoy, and let your imagination run wild!

@happeyside

@the_koo_koo_nest_

MAKING THE MOST OF YOUR SPACE

The dining area doesn't need to be a room with a big table and matching chairs like the ones you see in period dramas; it just has to be a space where you can gather with friends and family to eat, drink and socialise. We touch on open-plan living in the kitchen chapter, but let's look at this idea on a smaller scale.

@elm_terrace_interior   @oldflame1

You can easily create a little dining space where you can entertain guests in apartments or smaller kitchens. One of the best ways to do this is with a breakfast bar. This is a great asset as it can act as a worktop space as well as providing somewhere to sit, which is key when you need to utilise every inch of space. A breakfast bar is also a great way to divide the room into different zones, so you feel like you have a separate dining area.

"For my small apartment kitchen, I used wall cabinets as base cabinets to create a space-saving (and more cost-effective) breakfast bar. Since they're shallower, you can use a normal piece of worktop rather than a specially-made worktop." Jack

For those who live in rented homes and are unable to change the kitchen to accommodate a breakfast bar, or if you're looking for a budget-friendly option, consider introducing a high table and stools. These compact additions can easily fit in to an existing space. Look at how @gallowsgreen_reno has used a table and stools to create the perfect dining spot below. You could also invest in a small bistro table for two, as @acorn_cottage_ has done, perhaps with extra folding chairs for when guests come over. Built-in bench seating is great for storage, as well. There are lots of options!

@acorn_cottage_

@gallowsgreen_reno

@jackdmarch

@tale_of_a_terrace

THE PRACTICALITIES

Everyone wants their dining space to look fantastic, but it also needs to be practical and fit for purpose. Nothing beats having a few good-sized, clear surfaces where you can set down platters of delicious food when family and friends come over.

A dining room is a great place to use rich accents to give a sense of occasion, but we should be mindful not to choose anything so busy or overbearing that it interferes with anyone's culinary experience. Choosing a dining chair is on a par with choosing a bed: you want something that allows you to relax comfortably for a long period of time.

One of the best things about the dining room is that, since it centres around what is usually a quite sizeable, static piece of furniture, your choice of light fitting is fair game. The sky's the limit in terms of what you can choose to hang there. Because flow of traffic is forced around the table, there's limited risk of anyone crashing into what hangs above it (unless you're into dancing on tables). If you've ever longed for a statement light fitting, here's your chance to cash in!

"The best tables I've ever owned have been oval, and I would always choose a curve over a right angle where tables are concerned. Not only do I find them more sociable to sit at, you can also squeeze extra guests around them if the need arises." Wendy

@miltonmanor

@zephs_house

THE HOME BAR

Your dining area is also a great place to set up a home bar. There's been a huge resurgence in bar carts over the last few years, and the good news is that you can usually pick them up from online marketplaces, house clearance warehouses and antique or charity shops.

For most of us, staying in eventually becomes the new going out, especially if we're living under the constraints of a renovation budget. Creating a bar space within your dining area is a fab way to exercise your styling muscle by injecting some fun into what is also a practical storage solution.

Not everyone has the space to dedicate to a home bar, but here's a particularly impressive example to inspire you. @interiorcurve has achieved her ultimate party room, showcasing her signature flamboyant style.

@interiorcurve

OUTDOOR DINING

If you're lucky enough to have a garden, a paved yard or even a small balcony, creating a dedicated space for alfresco dining will make you feel like you've gained an extra room. It provides you with the perfect space to entertain guests when an outside gathering is preferred during the warmer months. How you design an outdoor dining area will depend on the space you have available, but a lack of square footage shouldn't prevent anyone from creating a beautiful place to sit and enjoy time outside. Undeterred by the size and shape of her balcony, Louise @dougs.digs has created a wonderful outdoor space by adding a palette sofa, a side table and a small number of simple accessories. Planters, an outdoor rug, cushions and bistro lighting help to create a wonderfully relaxing space.

@dougs.digs

@sallydoessassy

Anyone with a garden will be able to create a simple outdoor dining area, but with a little imagination you can go one step further and turn your space into several distinct 'rooms'. @sallydoessassy has created a wonderful, all-season dining and living area by covering her veranda with corrugated plastic. She zoned the areas by placing a dining table at one end and more relaxed lounge seating at the other. She further defined these zones with the use of plants and disco balls, and added a shelf to display objects of interest. This creates the feeling of outdoor rooms and a seamless extension of the house. The addition of sheepskin rugs, fire pits and bistro lighting will provide a dollop of *hygge* in the cooler autumnal months.

@sallydoessassy

@hardcastletower

As you can see, @hardcastletowers' compact paved yard didn't stop her from creating a beautiful haven for her family to enjoy.

"When my house was built in 1805, the garden was merely a place for the outside toilet and to tie up the horse. I think it's a bit of a stretch to call it a garden; it's more of a yard. I think it's small but beautifully formed. We have created an outside room that is an extension of our house, where we can eat and entertain friends in the summer. The use of furniture, rugs, cushions and other objects that aren't designed to be used outside creates the feeling of a luxurious space, and they can easily be tidied up at the end of the day. The walls and fences are all painted the same colour, and a pergola adds both height and privacy."
Joanne

Joanne has created zones so that her space has multiple functions. A pergola was erected to create welcome shade over the dining table and the open, uncovered area has comfier seating, creating a more informal space where people can relax. Outdoor shelving, mirrors and rugs all help to create the feeling of a real room.

It's also worth mentioning that if your garden has tired old flagstones, and replacing them isn't financially feasible, then there are ways to transform them beyond all recognition at very little cost. All it takes is a lick of paint, a stencil and a lot of elbow grease. Don't be put off by the thought of all that hard work; as you can see in @story_behind_the_stone's photographs below, the transformation is quite incredible. There are many tutorials online that offer a step-by-step process and show you how to achieve something similar.

@story_behind_the_stone

For those fortunate enough to have a large garden, the world is your oyster when it comes to outdoor living. When @sissinghurstlocationhouse bought her property, she not only inherited a substantial garden but also a derelict, sixty-foot Victorian greenhouse.

With enormous vision and a lot of hard work, Sally set about bringing this dilapidated but beautiful building into the twenty-first century. She painstakingly removed broken glass, weeds and debris and slowly transformed the greenhouse into the most breathtaking of outdoor spaces. Sally sought advice from professionals to establish the stability of the structure and, once she was reassured of its sturdiness, she added clear plastic sheeting to make it watertight so that it could be used all year round.

Beautifully styled, the chandeliers, candles and bistro lights add the all-important drama to give this outdoor space a show-stopping WOW factor.

All photos @sissinghurstlocationhouse

@househomo

TEN DINING ROOM COMMANDMENTS

1. Transform an everyday dining space with clever use of accessories such as tablecloths, seasonal foliage and pretty crockery.

2. Scour charity shops for interesting crockery to create an eclectic look.

3. Wall cabinets can be used as base cabinets and paired with a regular worktop to create a space-saving breakfast bar.

4. To maximise storage potential, consider bench seating. It's perfect for storing items you don't use every day.

5. Round or oval tables can work well in tight spaces and will accommodate extra seating.

6. Leave some surfaces clear so you have a place to put down platters and extra crockery.

7. Consider comfort when choosing dining chairs; your guests will appreciate it when they're seated for long periods.

8. Make the most of the space above the dining table and install a statement light fitting.

9. A small balcony can be transformed into an outdoor eating area with a little creativity.

10. Consider zoning sections of your garden to create outdoor living spaces.

@oldrectonewoldrec

THE KITCHEN

"The kitchen is the place I've spent many an evening sitting on the wooden worktop, cross-legged with a pot of tea, having a heart-to-heart with a friend sitting at the breakfast bar opposite me."
Jack

"Sharing food is one of life's great pleasures, so the kitchen is one of the most important rooms in my house. Having the time and space to prepare a meal is a true luxury."
Joanne

"The heart of the home."

"Fundamentally, I want my kids to remember this space as the safe haven of their childhood: a perpetually warm and comforting place where they could always find a family member."
Wendy

"I like to think of the kitchen as a family hub: the place where we gather to cook, eat and put the world to rights. Our kitchen is open plan so it's a noisy, sociable space – just the way I like it."
Maz

FORM AND FUNCTION

The kitchen is the hardest working room in the house, but who says a functional space has to be boring? Certainly not us! Never before has there been so much scope to showcase your personal style in the kitchen. As a busy, lively space where lots of activity takes place, the kitchen is the perfect room to take a risk with your décor and let your fun side shine through.

Shaker-style kitchens are enormously popular, but you can achieve a unique look by choosing a bold paint colour. Whether it's a moody palette for those who prefer the dark side, a bright pop for the colour-lovers or muted tones for those who champion the timeless and classic look, the options are endless. It's never been easier to give your kitchen a makeover; you're only ever a lick of paint away from a total transformation and a whole new style. If you aren't comfortable with the idea of painting your cabinets, there's an even easier and more budget-friendly option: simply change your handles to give the kitchen a fresh look.

@oakappledecor

"Aside from being a practical place where I love to cook, I hope that my children remember the kitchen as a perpetually warm and comforting space where they could flop down in a chair, fill their bellies and chat through any problems they have." Wendy

These farmhouse style kitchens evoke feelings of family; they provide a spacious area where everyone can sit and eat together. A central space like this is truly the heart of the home.

The main focus in a larger kitchen will usually be the table. Well-chosen seating and good lighting will encourage people to linger in the space, as they enjoy the ritual of preparing and sharing food. This English country inspired look can be achieved with a scrubbed, second-hand table and an eclectic mix of chairs, or by incorporating a kitchen island and smart bar stools. These options may be worlds apart budget-wise, but they are equally effective.

"As children we would always eat in the kitchen at a big, old, scrubbed pine farmhouse table; we each had our own chair, and they would wobble on the uneven quarry tiles beneath." Jack

@sissinghurstlocationhouse

Remember when kitchen appliances only ever came in white? Thankfully, those days are long gone: now you can find appliances in every hue from black to orange. There are styles to suit all budgets, and there are even paints available that will allow you to transform your white goods with a flick of a brush (there are lots of handy tutorials online explaining the process, and which products you'll need). Who wants a boring fridge when you can have a candy pink one?

Some people favour clean, simple lines and like their kitchenware to be hidden away in cupboards, whereas others believe in showing everything off on open shelving. In a world where every object can be beautiful as well as functional, why not have a little fun and make your kitchenalia a design choice? Open shelving is also a great way to maximise vertical space which can be critical in small kitchens. While we're on the subject of small kitchens, it can help to think of the ceiling as a fifth wall if space is really tight. Consider attaching hanging racks to your ceiling, to increase your storage space.

"Open shelving allows you to showcase every piece of stylish kitchenware you own. Yes, it does get dusty (that special kind of greasy dust which sticks like glue), but that's a small price to pay if you're the kind of person who likes to exhibit your wares." Joanne

"Having everything on show brings me deep joy. I can see things that I use on a daily basis, things I love and want to look at, and things which make me smile or evoke a fond memory." Joanne

The kitchen is also the ideal room to indulge in a bit of seasonal styling. A bottlebrush tree, a few artfully placed pumpkins or a vase of daffodils are all you need to change the vibe in your kitchen and give it a fresh look at any time of year.

1. @twyxhouse
2. @jackdmarch
3. @lifehasrepurpose

Since functionality is so important in the kitchen, let's consider the work triangle. Whether you're starting from scratch with your own design or deciding where best to house crockery and utensils in an existing space, it's a good idea to be aware of the active zone in the room – the space between the oven, the sink and the fridge. It's a good idea to engineer foot traffic away from the work triangle, if you can. Once you've established the work triangle in your own kitchen, you can start to position other pieces around it, according to your own personal style, space and budget. Think about where you will stand to prepare food and what you can see from that point. You may not be looking out of a window, but you can still create an attractive view for yourself using a favourite object or a display of flowers.

Floors are worth some serious consideration. Stone and hardwood are arguably the most durable, waterproof options, and can be replicated cost effectively in a variety of hard-wearing materials such as ceramic and vinyl. Tiles and splashbacks preserve any walls that are susceptible to splashes from food and liquids. @the_listed_home showcases a fabulous patterned tile opposite that would definitely disguise any saucy mishaps. If patterned tiles aren't your thing, metro tiles work brilliantly in contemporary or classic kitchens, as you can see with @thatonetrickpony below. In addition to thinking about aesthetics, you should also consider how often you're prepared to wipe your surfaces down. Anything with a high gloss finish will need regular buffing to restore its lustre, so matt may be the better choice for your lifestyle.

@paintthetownpastel   @thatonetrickpony

SPECIAL

@the_listed_home

Create a feature wall from the bare bones of your property and give it an industrial vibe with exposed brick. There are a range of sealants that will make a wall splash and dust proof if you are lucky enough to uncover some pretty brickwork. Alternatively, brick slip tiles are a great way to fake it.

@mamofboys

The kitchen is often considered to be a key social space, as well as a control centre from which the entire household operates. Gone are the days where guests were formally invited into a living or dining room; the kitchen is usually where it's at these days.

There are many ways to personalise an open-plan space and make it work for individual needs. A good starting point is to divide your kitchen into zones. These zones can then be defined by changing the flooring in different parts of the room, with the use of rugs, for example.

If you're looking for more definition and you have the space, you can further zone your kitchen through the use of furniture like open bookshelves. This is a great way to create the feeling of distinct rooms within the space, while still maintaining an open-plan aesthetic. Strategically placed plants, mirrors and artwork can also help to define an area and are very useful tools whatever the size of the room.

All photos @the_idle_hands

@negi.at.home

@projectsfromwaltonroad

Creating an open-plan living space doesn't necessarily involve extensive or costly building work. Many homes have achieved this simply by taking down an interior wall to open up the space. In @negi.at.home's traditional terraced house, the dining room was separate from the kitchen and was positioned at the back of the property. To create an open-plan feel, a wall was removed between the kitchen and the dining room, and patio doors were installed to allow light to flood the space. It is important to note that guidance should always be sought from an expert such as a structural engineer to ensure that walls can be removed without the need for additional structural support.

Size really doesn't matter when it comes to an open-plan layout. It's all about what you do with the available space, and this will determine how well the areas will work in practice. Christina @thisonefloats has created an open-plan living/kitchen area on a recently renovated 1960s barge. Her incredible creative vision has not only restored this boat but transformed it into a truly show-stopping home.

@thisonefloats

TEN KITCHEN COMMANDMENTS

1. If you're on a budget, start with small changes like a new paint colour or new hardware.

2. Inject fun pops of colour by choosing bright, bold appliances.

3. Open shelves are the perfect platform for you to inject some personality and style into your kitchen.

4. Use seasonal objects to add interest: try a bowl of lemons, a few artfully placed pumpkins or a Christmas mug.

5. Establish your work triangle first; if you get this right, everything else will come much more easily.

6. Think about where you will stand to prepare food and what you can see from that point, then create an attractive view.

7. Opt for a hardwearing and waterproof floor.

8. Consider using rugs to soften an area, or to help mark out a living or dining area in an open-plan kitchen.

9. A rug in an eye-catching texture or shape placed under a dining table will not only help to separate that area but will also add a bit of warmth.

10. Removing an interior wall can be an easy and cost-effective way to achieve a kitchen-diner.

@mrs_k_at_the_bridge

@susiebluesrooms

THE BEDROOM

"I realised how much I like stepping out of bed and feeling warm carpet under my toes during our reno when we lived with dusty floorboards everywhere for months on end."
Wendy

"People often say to me, 'How do you sleep in a room with so much going on?' To which I simply reply, 'All rooms are the same when you have your eyes closed!'"
Jack

"A place for rest, relaxation and romance."

"I adore bright colours and managed to find the perfect shade that is both soothing and relaxing. The deep teal makes me feel safe, almost as though I'm in a cocoon."
Joanne

"Less is definitely more when it comes to my idea of bedroom styling. My recipe for a great night's sleep is neutral décor, unpatterned bedding and a clutter free environment."
Maz

GO BOLD

There are definitely two camps when it comes to bedrooms, so if you don't fall into the 'neutral and serene' camp then you are most likely on the 'go bold, go dramatic, go to bed' team. Dramatic bedrooms have been around for centuries: cast your mind back to imposing, four-poster beds with yards of embroidered silk upholstery, surrounded by matching curtains, lampshades and rugs. But you don't have to go for a stately home vibe to create a dramatic room that reflects your personality and flexes your interior design skills. As you can see opposite, @evie_polkadot has created a bold, atmospheric bedroom with the use of dark walls. The space is lifted and given warmth through the clever use of jewel tones and gold accents.

Don't fear, though: if black walls aren't your thing, there are many other dramatic options, so you'll have no trouble finding one to suit your personality. Panelling is not only a great way to add depth and texture to a room, it also provides a surface on which to experiment with a bold paint colour. A small, panelled area in an otherwise neutral room will give you a space where you can dip your toe into the world of colour rather than plunging in headfirst.

"Don't be afraid to experiment with colour, especially when it comes to paint. As a child, my mum always used to say to me, 'you can soon paint over it again', and that's what she usually did! Our living room once changed colour three times in a month." Jack

1 2 3   1. @evie_polkadot, 2. @ourtaylormadehome, 3. @multicoloured.everything

@thepajaamahub

@interiorcurve

Wallpaper has always been a common sight in bedrooms. Its popularity peaked in the seventeenth century, with many influencers (yes, they had influencers back then as well) choosing to decorate in print and pattern. However, many people are scared of wallpaper as it's a big commitment. There's the fear of putting it up and getting the pattern repeat wrong, and then there's the question of how difficult it will be to remove when you fancy a change. Thankfully, there have been many clever advancements in wall coverings in the last few years, including removable papers and murals. This means there's plenty of scope to really give your room a punch with a bold pattern or print. Pro tip: a steam cleaner on the window setting makes a great wallpaper steamer if you do decide you're ready for a change.

If painting or embellishing the walls with papers and panelling isn't possible for you, there are still ways you can give your boudoir some dramatic impact. Patterned rugs, bright soft furnishings and a statement bed can help to create a bold and personal space.

A NEUTRAL PALETTE

It's not an exaggeration to say that getting the colours right in your bedroom can be the key to getting a good night's sleep. With this in mind, when designing your bedroom, choosing your colours is usually the best starting point.

A neutral palette is ideal if you want to create a sense of peace and tranquillity; many people find bright, saturated colours make them feel too alert and over-stimulated. Calming, neutral tones will provide a restful backdrop for more creative accents such as luxurious fabrics and feature headboards.

@coffee_beans_and_indigo_dreams

@justices_nest

@susiebluesrooms

When we consider neutral tones, we tend to think of beiges, whites and other pale colours, but darker options such as greys and blacks will also provide a feeling of peace and relaxation while adding drama to a space. Deep greys and black can work well in a small room because darker colours appear to recede, tricking the eye into thinking the walls are further away than they actually are. We might assume that they will make a space feel smaller when, in fact, they can have the opposite effect.

In smaller spaces it's often worth decorating the ceiling in a lighter shade than the walls so that the room doesn't feel too cave-like. This will help to create the illusion that the walls are taller and that the ceiling is higher.

If you want to create more impact, though, the ceiling (or 'fifth wall') can be painted in a darker colour to provide a dramatic backdrop for a statement light fitting.

1. @littleterracedhouseonthehill
2. @peartreecottagelife
3. @peartreecottagelife
4. @ginandinteriors

1
2 3 4

When choosing your colour scheme, it's wise to consider the aspect of the room. North-facing rooms tend to bring out the cooler tones within a colour, so opt for something with warmer hues. Rooms with a southern aspect will generally enjoy richer, warmer light, making them the easiest rooms to decorate. East or west-facing bedrooms will have sun in the morning and evening respectively, so choose a colour that will harness the natural light at its best.

CHILDREN'S BEDROOMS

"As a teenager, I would spend hours moving the furniture around and pinning pages ripped from magazines on the walls. It made me realise that my living space could reflect my personality, which is when my obsession with interiors first began. I vividly remember an article in a teen magazine where they had removed the doors from the wardrobes to make open shelf storage. Unfortunately, this was vetoed by my parents and so my design choice was thwarted, but it created an interiors itch that needed to be satisfied."
Joanne

"I've always been very particular about my bedroom décor. When I was nineteen, I moved to London and became a live-in nanny. I knew the day I rocked up that I would have to redecorate immediately. The colour palette was not to my taste; it looked like a unicorn had vomited rainbows using the 1990s rag-rolling effect."
 Maz

"As a child, I would spend hours during the school holidays decorating my playhouse at the bottom of the garden. It was everything from a cosy cottage to shops and museums; at one point it was even a New York loft apartment. Once I grew up a bit and my love for interiors had developed, my parents let me loose on my bedroom. My very first design choice, back in 2004, was a chocolate brown feature wall against a soft cream, with paw print stencils. What can I say: I loved dogs."
Jack

"I have come full circle on bedroom décor. I've had a four poster bed and sold it. I've had borders, wall transfers, warm terracotta, dark, patterned wallpaper… and I can finally declare that I've found my happy place: simple and tranquil."
Wendy

Often, your childhood bedroom is the first space that is really your own: a place where you can express your personality. But before a child gets to put their stamp on a room, their parents or carers have the responsibility of choosing the décor. Planning a nursery is a true privilege; for some people it's one of the most exciting room projects they will ever embark on. There is a primal instinct behind it: a need for it to be perfect for your new arrival.

Adaline

YOU
ARE
MY
SUN
SHINE

@justices_nest

@thiscolourfulnest

@housekidscats

Consider the psychology of colour before you break out the paint. Pink and coral are considered calming and soothing; they can actually lower the heart rate as they emulate the mother's womb. Yellow is said to stimulate intelligence, and green is thought to be the colour of harmony and balance. Red can be over-stimulating and blue can feel cold.

It's probably best to avoid adorning the walls in character wallpaper with matching bedding; a neutral background will last longer and can be accessorised with your dear darling's current fad of choice. The trend of painting murals, polka dots, scalloped edges and stripes is a cheap and easy way to add a fun element to the room.

@elizadarlings

CHILDREN'S BEDROOM STORAGE

Storage is a constant struggle in a children's bedroom. Although we would love to display wooden toys and pastel ragdolls in our best Scandi style, the rainbow plastic will always dominate the space. And books… there are so many books! Let's look at some clever ways to keep the room tidy and clutter-free.

Add shelving or fitted cupboards wherever there's space; make the most of any alcoves or other nooks and crannies. Store anything you want little hands to have easy access to on low shelves and place more ornamental things safely out of reach on higher shelves.

@coral.atkinson

Locker-style cabinets are durable and will hide a multitude of things. And don't forget the space under the bed: shallow boxes on casters can provide the perfect home for building bricks and barbie dolls, allowing you to tidy the room with ease.

Older children and teens will need somewhere to work, and very possibly somewhere to spend hours perfecting their hair and make-up technique, too. Running a worktop along one wall creates a perfect space for this, and there's the added bonus of plenty of storage space underneath. A gallery wall dedicated to their favourite celeb idols will save them sticking posters up and ruining the walls.

Bunk beds are ideal for children sharing a room, or as a spare bed for sleepovers. A loft bed is a fabulous way to gain extra floor space or to create a cosy den, quiet desk space or fun dressing-up area.

@twopigsonehouse

CREATING A RESTFUL SPACE

There's a lot to consider when furnishing your bedroom. The aim is to make it as restful a space as you possibly can, so anything that compromises comfort or assaults the senses has got to go! Yes, a sleigh bed or something with a footboard may look striking, but it won't be very practical if you're over six feet tall. Think about what works for you as well as what looks good. In general, neutral, calming tones create a peaceful haven that you'll look forward to walking in to.

@martinas_cosy_crib

@tale_of_a_terrace

Some people like to wake naturally as the sun rises and light floods the room. If you're not one of those people, black-out blinds shut out summer mornings when you're trying your hardest to eke out a lie-in; they can also keep out the dark nights when winter comes and you want to hunker down. Sheer voile panels work well for when none of the above applies, and they're also a great way to ensure privacy if you happen to be overlooked.

Double-glazed windows act as a great barrier to both cold and sound. If your property has single-glazed panels, you will benefit from heavy, interlined window dressings, which have excellent thermal properties that keep the room cosy in the colder months while also absorbing sound. This is particularly important during summer when we tend to have windows open and are more likely to fall victim to noise pollution from activity outside. Fixing a weatherproof strip across the bottom of your bedroom door will help combat unwanted noise travelling in from a hallway. A piece of heavy or fitted furniture is a great solution to buffer sound and cold from outside or adjoining walls.

According to Feng Shui experts, it's a good idea to keep clutter to a minimum in the bedroom, and that includes inside wardrobes and drawers. So, it stands to reason that even if it's a multi-purpose room, materials related to work should be banned; we want to associate this room with a restorative night's sleep, not the stresses of the day. It's also been said that the main focus in this room should be yourself (and your partner if you have one). So, move those family portraits to another room and keep the photos of your friends out of there, too!

@asmalltownhouse

@peartreecottagelife

TEN BEDROOM COMMANDMENTS

1. Neutral tones will provide a calm, restful environment.

2. Dark colours can work well in small areas because they trick the eye into thinking the walls are further away.

3. Think about the aspect of the bedroom and choose a colour that will harness the natural light at its best.

4. Consider the psychology of colour in relation to the mood you want to achieve.

5. When decorating a child's room, don't be influenced by fads: opt for a more neutral, timeless design that will last beyond their latest obsession.

6. Optimise alcoves, nooks and crannies for storage.

7. Think about your practical needs, not just about what looks good.

8. Black-out window coverings keep out bright mornings.

9. Keep clutter to a minimum to help encourage a restorative night's sleep.

10. You and your partner (if you have one) should be the main focus in this room. Keep family or group portraits elsewhere.

@making_walford_magical

THE BATHROOM

"Bathrooms have come a long way from the ones I remember as a child. Gone are the days of the rubber shower attachment, carpet up the side of the bath and a bottle of Mr Matey balanced on the side."
Joanne

"I'm not a big watcher of television so the bathroom is probably the most important room in my house. It's a cosy sanctuary from the outside world, but then I am a self-confessed bath lover and wallowing champion."
Jack

"A sanctuary to relax and escape."

"I'm currently designing two bathrooms, but I find this room the trickiest to plan because mistakes can't be rectified quickly or cheaply. I'm aiming to create something timeless that I'll still be happy with in five years."
Maz

"I'm unapologetically a shower person. I've tried so many times to get into bathing. I'd love to love it but I just don't. I can appreciate a beautiful looking bath but I'm a shower girl through and through."
Wendy

THE BASICS

Size does matter when it comes to a bathroom because the space you have available will have a big impact on the design possibilities. But creative storage solutions and a few high-end finishes will ensure that even the smallest of bathrooms can deliver serious wow factor. If you're lucky enough to have a large bathroom space, there are countless design possibilities. Feature baths, separate walk-in showers, twin basins, large storage cupboards… the list is endless. For many of us, though, the bathroom is the smallest room in the property, so it's important that it's designed to suit the people who live there and reflects their needs.

When it comes to planning a smaller bathroom, it helps to identify what type of bather you are. For some people, the bathroom is a sanctuary: a place to relax, unwind and literally soak away the worries. For others, it's purely a functional space to take a quick shower; they prefer to retreat to other areas of the home for their R&R. If you're one of those people who falls into the first category then your bath is key. If the size of your bathroom won't accommodate a separate shower then you'll need an over-the-bath shower; they have come a long way, and attractive shower screens are plentiful. Whether you prefer plain glass or Crittall, there is something for everyone.

@ahousetomakeourhome

@story_behind_the_stone

@hardcastletowers

@projectreno14

You may like to try the same approach as @hardcastletowers and opt for a shower curtain that can be kept out of sight when dry. Whatever your preference, remember to keep the look as minimal as possible in order to open up the space in a smaller bathroom.

For those of you who view a bathroom as somewhere to wash and go then maybe you need to ask yourself if you really need that bath. Do you have a young family? If the answer is no, then losing the bath in favour of a huge walk-in shower could be a better option. As it's relatively cheap and easy to install a bath these days, the likelihood is that a potential buyer won't be deterred by the lack of one, and it wouldn't be too costly to install one for a quick sale should your estate agent advise it.

@thegirlwiththegoldensofa

MAKING THE MOST OF YOUR SPACE

Once you've decided what's going into your bathroom, there are some design choices that will help create the illusion of more space.

Mirrors are one of the best ways to open up a room as they reflect light into darker areas. Light, bright, reflective surfaces will also help to create the illusion of space. A clear glass panel will work better than a shower curtain as the eye won't register that it's dividing up your space.

Consider using recessed shelving as a space saver. Pipework can be hidden behind false walls, so ask a builder to use some of this space to create recessed shelving. This design feature can be particularly useful in the shower as it gives you somewhere within easy reach to store all the essentials.

Wall-mounted mixer taps work well in small bathrooms, since pipework is hidden and therefore a pedestal is not required. The space you save can be used for essential storage with the addition of some shelving or drawers.

@85_wf

@holly_homestyle

@the_listed_home

Wall-mounted basins and shelving also help to create the illusion of more space in smaller bathrooms. By lifting these bulky items off and away from the floor, it makes the room feel larger. You can also opt for a ledge or shelf above a basin so essentials such as toothpaste and soap are to hand. It's also nice to have somewhere to showcase prettier bathroom knick-knacks. The wall behind the toilet is often redundant, so this could be a good place to install a few pretty, space-saving shelves to display more decorative items.

THE FINER DETAILS

Not all of us are blessed with multiple bathrooms, and those of us who dwell in a smaller house or flat may only have one hard-working bathroom to serve the whole household. Of course, it has to be a functional space, but that doesn't mean it can't exude style and personality. What you need to do is create the right balance between a practical space and a luxurious sanctuary.

There are many ways you can inject style and personality into your bathroom. You've probably noticed that bath boards are back in fashion, and these are the perfect way to spruce up your bathroom if you're on a budget or live in a rented home and are unable to change your bathroom suite. There are many bath boards available to purchase, but you can also repurpose an old board and create your own. They can be accessorised with mood-enhancing candles, and they're the perfect place to balance your G&T, book or e-reader.

"It's all about finding the middle ground; it doesn't have to be functional over fabulous." Jack.

The humid atmosphere in a bathroom can be ruinous to regular paint and wallpaper, but you can treat wallpaper with a clear matt varnish to stop it being spoiled. Although you can get special waterproof bathroom paint, the most practical solution has got to be tiles. The floor must be durable enough to withstand toddlers splashing, leaking pipes, damp towels being strewn around and whatever else your family throws at it. However, humidity also creates the ideal environment for plants. You can make space for some greenery in even the tiniest of bathrooms: they can be squeezed into tight corners or hung from the ceiling.

@bungalow_fifty8

@squid_and_goose

@making_walford_magical

Storage is one of the hardest problems to overcome, since bathrooms are often small spaces, so you'll need to think outside the box if you want to make it look good. Remember that you aren't limited to furniture and accessories that have been specially designed for the bathroom: old pieces of regular furniture can be repurposed, baskets can be attached to the wall with hooks and screws and hat boxes and cases can be stacked in a corner.

Decanting shampoos and shower gels into more attractive glass bottles will give the room a more coordinated feel and elevate the space into something a little more special. You can use anything from vintage bottles picked up in second-hand shops or old recycled bottles to cut glass decanters.

@susiebluesrooms

@nido_uk

@susiebluesrooms

BATHROOM MAKEOVERS

You shouldn't be daunted by the prospect of giving your bathroom a makeover; it isn't necessary to replace the entire bathroom suite to give the room a new lease of life. Think smaller if you need to: consider updating the taps, replacing the bath panel and changing the colour scheme either by getting new accessories or changing your wall colours. Dated tiles can be tackled with tile transfers which can be sourced online, and you can even create bespoke designs using materials like car vinyl. A bathroom makeover really can be tailored to any budget.

"It came to me one day while I was at work, ordering vinyl stickers for a loan car. I thought, if these will stay on the car through sunshine and rain then surely they will stay on a tile through a steamy shower!" Jack

@annalysejacobs

@jackdmarch

Another great way to refresh a bathroom is with a flick of a paintbrush and a mini roller. With the help of some waterproof bathroom paint and a few online tutorials, you'll be able to transform a tired roll top into a super chic statement bath. Whether you opt for a bright pop of yellow or a muted tone, this simple step can totally transform the space.

1 2 3
4 5 6
7 8 9

1. @heneddyhouse   2. @myedwardianhouse   3. @thenuthouseuk   4. @nortonvillas   5. @postprentisdesign
6. @casamiadellfield   7. @lara.bezzina   8. @moveovermagnolia   9. @this_somerset_farmhouse

COLOURS AND TEXTURES

For those living in flats and apartments, it's common for bathrooms to be windowless and lacking in natural light. In cases like this, it's best to keep the colour palette light and use spotlights to give you as much light as possible.

Natural colours and textures work well in all bathrooms. Just take a look at spas and hotel rooms; they're the perfect places to get inspiration. If you visit a spa, you'll see plenty of luxurious but versatile finishes that withstand water, soap and steam, all while creating the calming sanctuary feel that many of us crave. If you're in the fortunate position of being able to remodel your entire bathroom, you could also take inspiration from the way hotels and spas use lighting to create ambience. You can achieve something similar at home by zoning lights across different switches.

@fig_tart

Generally speaking, a hotel bathroom is small and designed to maximise space, so it can be a useful template for redesigning your own bathroom. Take note of the way the pieces are arranged and how storage has been incorporated, then think about how you can apply these clever strategies to your own bathroom.

This bath from @fig_tart is the epitome of luxe and makes a real statement.

CHOOSING TILES

Tile samples tend to be quite small, so making this key design choice can be a daunting prospect, especially when you begin to reach the top end of your budget. But there are other ways to help you decide. It can be a good idea to snap a few pictures of any interesting bathrooms you find yourself visiting; don't be afraid to photograph great tiles if you spot them in a nice restaurant bathroom! These spaces are often created by designers to have a visual impact and it's a great opportunity to see how a bold choice of wall or floor covering will work. A sample of the fabulous floor in @milestone_cottage's bathroom below would only give a small indication of what the finished pattern would look like.

A great way to make a tiled surface pop is to use coloured grout. Where lighter-coloured grout has become discoloured or stained, an easy and budget-friendly way to freshen it up is to use a grout pen. If your tile is not a standard shape, it will further enhance the pattern as a point of interest. Don't hesitate to factor underfloor heating into a bathroom if the opportunity arises, too. A hot fluffy towel is bliss, but the feeling of a warm floor underfoot, in a room where you're likely to spend a substantial amount of time in your birthday suit is nothing short of luxury, particularly on a chilly morning! As we can see below, by using a darker-coloured grout, @dustsheets_and_decor has tied her patterned bathroom floor and wall finish together and made the metro tiles pop. By continuing under the raised bath, she cleverly creates the illusion of extra floor space, too.

@milestone_cottage

@dustsheets_and_decor

@the_yorkshire_homestead

@watsons_at_westbornelodge

"I remember telling my sister that I intended to use a heavily veined marble on the floor and walls of our main bathroom. She was absolutely appalled, but eventually admitted that the finished effect was striking." Wendy

If you're planning to use real marble in your bathroom, you might want to look into 'book matching'. This is an amazing process where a slab of marble is sliced in such a way that the leading edges align to make a breathtaking symmetrical pattern. You can get ceramic versions of natural stone as a realistic and economical alternative, although it's definitely worth seeing what the repeat pattern of a typical box will be so that you're not going to see an obvious repeat every time you enter your newly tiled room. Above, we can see authentic-looking marble effect tiles in @watsons_at_westbornelodge's ensuite bathroom.

Another excellent way of introducing marble into your bathroom without blowing the bank is to use penny mosaics; these can be a little tricky to lay but are completely worth the investment and effort when you see the finished result.

TEN BATHROOM COMMANDMENTS

1. A large mirror will open up a small room as it reflects the light.

2. A clear glass panel will give the illusion of more space.

3. Bath boards can revive a tired bathroom suite and act as a useful storage solution.

4. Wallpaper can be used in the bathroom; just seal it with a layer of appropriate varnish.

5. Be creative with your storage and think outside the box.

6. Tiles can be given a new lease of life with use of tile paints or tile transfers.

7. It's a good idea to wire lighting on different switches so that you can alter the ambience in the room.

8. Using grout that's darker than your tiles is a great way to update a bathroom and disguise tired or discoloured areas.

9. Underfloor heating is an efficient way to heat a small bathroom and saves the space that a radiator might take up.

10. Mosaic or patterned tiles or vinyl on the floor of a small bathroom will help to create the illusion of space.

@onealchemyhouse

@21_holmfield

THE OFFICE

"My partner works from home, so the office is a vital space for us. It's somewhere to hide the chaos and contain all things work-related, so it's great for our work-life balance; when the door closes, the working day is over."
Jack

"I don't need much space: just a desk with a comfortable chair, a nice view and room for my sizable pen collection. The icing on the cake would be a door so I could lock everybody out."
Joanne

"A comfortable and well-planned area, tailored to maximise productivity."

"Our study is one of my favourite rooms. I don't allow a TV in there so it's not somewhere the children like to hang out. This means I can usually guarantee peace and quiet while I'm working."
Maz

"When I think of what a study should be, the first thing that comes to mind is an organised and clutter-free space, but if I'm entirely honest, our home office fits into neither of those categories."
Wendy

FIRST THINGS FIRST

There are many factors to consider when planning a home office. First, think about who the space is for and which other roles they might play within the household over the course of their working day. If a desk area is going to be used by various members of the family to perform daily admin and assignments, a central command station might be the answer. If the office is going to be used by one person and they are fulfilling a corporate role, it might be necessary to choose a quieter spot, away from the distractions of the main house.

When choosing your desk, it's important to think about the kind of work you do. If you need a lot of space to spread out papers or documents, you'll need a large surface to accommodate that. If all your work can be accessed electronically, a small work station that fits a laptop, a phone and a drink will suffice. If work needs to be packed away at the end of each day, you should factor this into your plan when it comes to storage, but if your paperwork has to stay out, you'll need an independent workspace that can remain undisturbed.

When you're spending a lot of time working from home, you need to make sure your physical environment is as comfortable as possible. If your workspace is located in a room with a window (which is ideal), you'll need to consider the position of your screen. Ideally, laptops and computers need to face away from windows to avoid reflections from the light, but being near natural light can also help you stay alert. Sheer panels, blinds or shutters will help to combat glare if you can't avoid having your screen facing a window. You may also find overhead, artificial lighting a hindrance as it can cause eye strain, so you may want to opt for a desk lamp instead. Think about your view, as well; if your only option is to face a wall, a piece of your favourite artwork will give you something cheery to look at.

@bananashed_home

@rockthishome

@home.plants.and.three.cats

@designermumetc

If your office is in a bedroom, consider whether installing a desk in a wardrobe or cupboard is a possibility. It's very important that work-related items are out of sight in this room; the focus should be on rest. Being able to shut the door on your work will help you to shut off and relax.

Due to recent events, better internet connections and flexible working policies, more people than ever are working from home, at least some of the time. Finding a suitable space where you can concentrate and get work done is now a common problem. Whatever your situation, it's about making the space you have work harder and being creative with what you've got.

The photo on the opposite page shows how @designermumetc makes valuable use of the often-forgotten space under the stairs. If you're struggling to find a desk to fit in an awkward spot, you could try running a worktop along the wall instead. Overhead lighting plus a desk lamp will create enough light to enable you to work comfortably in even the darkest of corners.

The photo on this page shows how @theplyhouse has cleverly created a study area inside her children's wardrobe, meaning that all desk paraphernalia can be hidden away when the desk is not in use.

"As a child we had a big cupboard, almost like a wardrobe, but when you opened its big double doors it had bookshelves, drawers and even a pull-out desk!" Jack

"I find working at the dining table means I get distracted, and I don't enjoy having to clear away my things when I've finished. Now I have a beautiful bureau – a bargain buy from a charity shop – tucked in a little corner. I attacked it with chalk paint, gave it fancy new knobs and now it's the perfect space to store all my work-related paraphernalia. My dining room no longer feels like a work space at the end of every day." Joanne

Whatever room you work in, introducing clever storage options will mean you can tidy away at the end of the day, so it doesn't feel like you're sleeping or eating in your workspace. If a cupboard isn't an option, there are many attractive storage solutions that will help you to hide your work equipment when it isn't in use. Vintage trunks and drawers can be repurposed so that your laptop and paperwork can be easily tidied away. You could also make use of a screen to help zone the space and separate the work area from the rest of the room.

@vintagecuratorinteriors

@the_little_pink_nest

good
vibes

NEW YORK
A PHOTOGRAPHIC ALBUM

LAS VEGAS

CENTURY

@housemouse_farmhouse

OFFICE ACCESSORIES AND STYLING

Ensuring that you have all your office accessories to hand will help you to be more effective. Open shelving is a great idea as it allows easy access to frequently used items, but if you're prone to hoarding then your clutter may be best hidden away behind a cupboard door. Even for those of us with the luxury of a dedicated home office, it's often the smallest room in the property, so space is always at a premium. It's a good idea to think outside the box when it comes to creative storage solutions in smaller rooms. Opt for high shelving to maximise the wall space available, or think about placing a shelf around a doorway so you're using part of the wall that would normally be redundant.

@squid_and_goose

@danisdomain

A noticeboard is a great place to display your targets and deadlines, and there are lots of ways to get creative when designing one. Adhesive cork tiles can be arranged in fun patterns to create a noticeboard without making holes in your walls. Chalkboard and magnetic paint can be applied directly to an area of wall, and documents can be displayed using magnets. Modular panels from office supply stockists can be fixed together onto a wall, while a wire noticeboard brings an industrial edge to this practical accessory.

@marta_at_the_mill

@miafelce

If you need to print, scan or shred documents, it makes sense for these devices to be within easy reach. If they'll be sitting out on your desk, make sure that you tidy away any cables so that you avoid creating a trip hazard. Wires can be discreetly attached to the leg of your workstation and you can buy various trunking solutions to keep multiple cables in check.

When it comes to that all-important styling, a lot of people find that a clean and simple working environment is best for them as it helps to avoid any distractions. But that doesn't mean your office needs to be a boring space; after all, every office needs practical storage solutions and this provides you with the perfect opportunity to implement some style.

@thepajaamahub

THE HOME LIBRARY

Most bibliophiles will require a decent amount of book storage, and the home office is a great location for this. Those without an office could utilise space in a hallway or living area instead, simply by running bookshelves along a wall. Creating a home library will add depth to a room, and a wall of books will provide a show-stopping feature for any home. Built-in book storage is a good way to make the most of the space available, and can be created on a budget with the use of materials such as MDF. Using a strong colour choice on the shelving will create a fabulous, high-end look. For those hard-to-reach shelves, consider incorporating a beautiful library ladder as @myedwardianhouse has done here.

@myedwardianhouse

@queen_of_mdf

@theplyhouse

"I'm a book hoarder, so, after the desk, one of my biggest requirements was book storage, and a lot of it. Our study is a narrow room, so by building up and around a doorway at the end of the room we were able to maximise the space we had." Maz

If space allows, most bookworms will welcome the addition of some cosy, comfy seating in their home library. After all, where better to put your feet up and enjoy the latest blockbuster than amongst a much-loved book collection?

Why not go one step further and take a leaf out of @queen_of_mdf and @theplyhouse's style books? Colour-coding your book collection will add a cheerful rainbow aesthetic to the room. Of course, this system might frustrate Dewey Decimal fans who prefer to arrange their books in a more logical order. There's no right or wrong way to arrange books, just choose a system that works for you.

@ahometomakeyousmile

TEN OFFICE COMMANDMENTS

1. Consider the surface area you need when choosing a desk or workstation.

2. Situate your desk so that the screen is facing away from the window. Sheer panels on your windows will combat glare on your screen.

3. Think about the available space and how you can make it work harder for you.

4. Clever storage options will mean that you can tidy away at the end of the day.

5. Position office accessories within easy reach of your workspace.

6. Consider using redundant wall space to create extra shelving or storage.

7. Get creative with your noticeboard. There are many different products that you can use to create the perfect spot to display your important dates, targets and information.

8. Take care of wires to avoid a trip hazard.

9. Choose seating that you find comfortable for long periods of time.

10. Create a cosy reading nook with a comfy chair and book shelving.

THANK YOU

Our thanks to everyone who contributed a photo of their beautiful home and made this book possible. As the founder members of the Story Of My Home hashtag, we look forward to seeing the interiors community thrive as it passes through the hands of its future custodians. We hope you enjoyed an insight into what can be achieved in your own spaces. Trends will always evolve but the real art of making a home is to find your own style and follow it unashamedly.